God's Pathway
to Healing

BONE HEALTH

BOOKS BY
REGINALD B. CHERRY, M.D.

GOD'S PATHWAY TO HEALING:

Bone Health

Diabetes

Digestion

Heart

Herbs That Heal

The Immune System

Joints and Arthritis

Memory and Mental Acuity

Menopause

Prostate

Vision

Vitamins and Supplements

Dr. Cherry's Little Instruction Book

God's Pathway
to Healing
BONE HEALTH

by

Reginald B. Cherry, M.D.

BETHANYHOUSE
Minneapolis, Minnesota

God's Pathway to Healing: Bone Health
Copyright © 2003
Reginald B. Cherry, M.D.

Manuscript prepared by Rick Killian, Killian Creative,
Boulder, Colorado. *www.killiancreative.com*

Cover design by Danielle White

Note: The directions given in this book are in no way to be
considered a substitute for consultation with your own
physician.

Published by Bethany House Publishers
11400 Hampshire Avenue South
Bloomington, Minnesota 55438

Bethany House Publishers is a Division of
Baker Book House Company, Grand Rapids, Michigan.

Printed in the United States of America

ISBN 0-7642-2836-6

CONTENTS

INTRODUCTION

There are 206 bones in our body, which make up the framework for our muscles, organs, nerves, arteries, veins, and other tissues. Just to take a single step we use sixty-two bones; imagine the coordination of bone movements we use to drive a car, do housework, swing a golf club, walk up or down stairs, or even reach for something on a high shelf! This skeletal framework is what holds us together—and in contrast, if it is weakened, we begin to slowly fall apart. Imagine the effect of that on our daily activities.

Throughout your lifetime, your body is continually breaking down old bone and building new bone. As you age, the building process slows down and doesn't keep up with the breaking-down process; thus, our bones become more porous and brittle. This can promote a disease called osteoporosis—literally, "porous bones"—and this can cause fractures in the spinal column, hips, wrists, and other places, which can diminish height, cause stooping, and even result in death from various complications. Osteoporosis strikes with little warning—too often its victims don't know they have it until they have already suffered serious damage from it. Statistics show that we are all susceptible to the disease, especially as we live longer, and we should take precautions to prevent it. Keeping our bones healthy may well be one of the best ways to maintain quality of life as we grow older, as strong bones enable us to stay active and mobile in spite of our years.

According to the National Osteoporosis Foundation, an estimated 10 million Americans suffer from osteoporosis already, while another 34 million are showing signs of reduced bone mass, one of the early indicators of the development of osteoporosis. This number represents 55 percent of those over the age of fifty, 80 percent of whom are women. One in two Caucasian women over the age of fifty either has osteoporosis or has had a bone fracture due to reduced bone mass. In fact, by age sixty-five, most women have lost from 30 to 50 percent of their bone mass. However, while osteoporosis is often considered a disease of the old, it can actually strike at any age. Nationally, we spent $17 billion in 2001 to treat this affliction, and osteoporosis was responsible for approximately 1.5 million bone fractures—that's more than 4,000 fractures a day.[1] It is estimated that by the year 2010, roughly 52 million people will be affected by bone disease, and by 2020 that number will climb to over 61 million.[2]

While some of us have more risk factors than others for developing osteoporosis, we can all take steps to prevent it. If we do a few simple things and have regular medical checkups, there is no reason that any of us needs to suffer any of the complications caused by this condition.

It is important to note that new information about bone disease shows why traditional treatments for poor bone health have not been successful. We now know that simply "throwing calcium" at our bones does not make them stronger. Our body needs several other nutrients along with calcium, and not all forms of calcium have the same effect. Obtaining more reliable information about this is crucial.

It is not God's plan that we should be crippled by bone disease as we grow older. I believe this is why He has revealed to us the things He put into creation to help us keep strong bones to the end of our days. If you are concerned about bone health—and from the statistical data, we all should be—please read this book carefully, discuss with your personal physician how the information here might be used to help you keep strong bones, and prayerfully follow the leading of the Holy Spirit as you pursue God's plan for you for healthy living.

—Reginald B. Cherry, M.D.

Chapter 1

GOD HAS A PATHWAY TO HEALTHY BONES FOR YOU

Chapter 1

GOD HAS A PATHWAY TO HEALTHY BONES FOR YOU

Then Peter said, Silver and gold have I none; but such as I have give I thee: In the name of Jesus Christ of Nazareth rise up and walk. And he took him by the right hand, and lifted him up: and immediately his feet and ankle bones received strength. (Acts 3:6–7)

Our God is a healing God, and He

works in many different ways to bring that
healing to us. Here in the book of Acts, a
man received renewed strength to his bones
through a request made in the name of Jesus.
In other places, Jesus combined natural substances with healing power to bring about a
miracle; or He told someone to do something, and when that person obeyed, he was
healed. In this modern era, I believe God is
revealing, through medical research, answers
that have not been available to other gener-
ations, in order to bring healing to us. The
key is to get good, reliable information and
then prayerfully follow it so that God can
lead you down the best pathway to healing
for you.

To find God's best pathway to healing or
avoiding bone disease, we need to combine
natural knowledge with supernatural wisdom

and faith. Sometimes this will bring about a quick healing, as with the man mentioned in the verse above who sat at the temple gate, and sometimes it will take some extra time and effort.

It is like the story of the blind man who came to Jesus for healing in the ninth chapter of John. Jesus did not heal him immediately. Instead, Jesus instructed him to follow a series of steps. He mixed clay with His saliva and put it on the man's eyes, but the man was not healed immediately. Jesus told him in effect, "I want you to find the pool at Siloam. When you come to it, I want you to wash this mud off. When you have done this, you will see again."

The man didn't argue. He didn't say, "Well, you know, I don't really believe in this kind of thing. I don't think clay and saliva

can heal a man's eyes. I'm not of that school
of thought." If you are reading this book,
you might say something like, "If Jesus
wants to heal me, He has the power to do
so. I don't think I need to take any medicine." This makes perfect sense, but often
God is looking more for obedience and
humility than to perform a spectacular miracle. Often we look for the spectacular and
miss the real miracle. Now, God would
never afflict you with a disease to get you to
obey or to be humble, but Satan might prick
your pride and stubbornness to keep you
from seeking out the help you need—the
help God wants you to have—to receive your
healing.

The way Jesus healed the blind man is
unique in the Scriptures. Nowhere else do
we read that Jesus put mud, or any other

substance, on someone and then told him to go wash it off in a pool in order to be healed. But the Bible says that the blind man went to the pool and washed the mud off and came away seeing (John 9:7). We should not be as concerned with the method as with the healing. We should leave the method up to God. Thank God that He can heal instantaneously, but let us be thankful, too, that He also provides other pathways to healing for us. This man's pathway was not instantaneous, but it was still miraculous.

When Jesus touched Bartimaeus to heal his blindness (Mark 10), I'm sure Bartimaeus appreciated not having mud put on his eyes, although the man in John 9 certainly didn't argue with Jesus. He didn't say, "Why did you put this stuff on my face? You didn't do that to Bartimaeus! Why did you treat me differently?" No, he didn't question Jesus' actions. He simply obeyed—and he was healed.

Many medical professionals will tell us that damage done to bones due to fractures resulting from bone-density loss and osteoporosis cannot be reversed, but breakthroughs in medical science are being made every day. And God is not limited to working through medical science to heal us, but He often uses this pathway to healing. It is also true that for some situations or conditions God alone has the solution. If we are to live by faith, as God has commanded us in His Word, we need to be open to His leading and follow His guidance. It is my belief that much of the material in this book has been revealed so that we can take steps to prevent bone disease by using self-discipline and wisdom. It is my prayer that as you prayerfully read the following chapters you will begin the journey down God's pathway to healing for you.

Chapter 2

OSTEOPOROSIS: THE SILENT DISEASE

Chapter 2

OSTEOPOROSIS: THE SILENT DISEASE

God's design is that we would have strong bodies and bones to the end of our days. Even modern science is beginning to question why we deteriorate as quickly as we do when evidence suggests that living to age 120 shouldn't be that odd of an occurrence—in some pockets of the world reaching beyond 100 is far from unusual. Yet somehow before we get even close to this age, most of us start to deteriorate and eventually die because of some complication or another. Most research in the area of longevity has been focused on diet and nutrition. In other words, the belief that a long, full life is more connected to diet and lifestyle than medications or health care is slowly changing the way medical science views its mission: We are slowly seeing the pendulum swing from an emphasis on treatment to an emphasis on prevention.

Such is definitely the case with bone disease and osteoporosis because of its invisible nature. Since we can neither see nor feel our bone density decreasing, the decline generally goes without notice until we break a bone or crush a vertebra. Fractures of the vertebrae are actually the most common type of fracture due to osteoporosis, making up roughly 700,000 of the 1.5 million fractures—nearly half—that occur annually. Because medical science is only recently discovering ways of repairing such fractures in the backbone, the result is generally a permanent reduction in height or stooping. With this, as with most other ailments, the old saying "An ounce of prevention is worth a pound of cure" is still very true. Whatever age we are, we need to make changes now to avoid health problems tomorrow.

However, before we talk about prevention, it is always a good idea to get a basic understanding of the problem we are facing so that when we are presented with the solution, we better understand how it works and are thus more likely to stay with it. For this reason, I would like to take some time here to briefly explain what osteoporosis is, what the risk factors are, complications of bone mass loss, and how you can detect it before it results in bone damage.

HOW ARE BONES BUILT UP
OR TORN DOWN?

Typically our bone development peaks at around thirty to thirty-five years of age. When we're young, new bone is not only being formed, but old bone is being systematically replaced at a rate of about 5 to 10 percent a year in a process called *bone remodeling*. In other words, old bone cells are eliminated and replaced with new ones. This process is regulated by the actions of vitamin D and certain hormones, including estrogen in women and testosterone in men, progesterone, calcitonin, and thyroid.

This bone remodeling happens as a function of the two different kinds of bone cells: osteoblast cells and osteoclast cells. Osteo-*blast* cells are in high gear from birth to age thirty as they build and replace bone. Osteo-*clast* cells, on the other hand, are responsible for detecting older or fatigued bone and tearing it down to be replaced.

Throughout the earlier years, the osteoblast cells (think *blast* or *b* for builder) outwork the osteoclast cells as bone grows and more bone is built than torn down. As we reach the age of thirty to thirty-five, this process balances out, and an equilibrium of building and tearing down is maintained for about ten more years. Then, depending on nutrition and a number of other factors, the osteoblast or "builder" cells begin to function less and less effectively, while the osteoclast cells continue to dismantle bone for regeneration. If this continues without intervention, eventually bone mass is so depleted that fractures can occur more and more easily. Bones become more honey-combed or porous, and this continues until it results in osteoporosis.

RISK FACTORS FOR OSTEOPOROSIS

A number of factors, some of which are hereditary and others of which are lifestyle choices, can indicate how likely a person is to develop osteoporosis. If we make the choice to change what we can and to com-pensate for those things that we cannot, we can minimize and avoid bone loss.

The major risk factors that you cannot change are:

- *Gender:* Women in general have less

bone mass than men, and this is further accentuated as women reach menopause and their production of estrogen drops. Estrogen helps in the bone-producing function of osteoblast cells, and as estrogen decreases, osteoblast cells lose an important ally in their fight to keep our bones strong. Women can lose 20 percent of their bone mass in the five to seven years after the onset of menopause. Men experience a similar bone loss as their testosterone levels drop, but men's testosterone levels do not drop nearly as much as women's estrogen levels do.

- *Menopause or menstrual history:* The early onset of menopause (either naturally or due to surgery) also increases the risk of bone mass loss and osteoporosis. Women who experience amenorrhea—a condition during which women have prolonged periods of time when they do not menstruate prior to menopause—are also at a higher risk.

- *Preexisting health issues:* Women with a history of bulimia, anorexia, malabsorption syndrome, or chronic kidney disease and those on thyroid medication or with an overactive thyroid are all at an increased risk because of poor calcium absorption into their bones earlier in life. They also tend to have lower estrogen output because of their reduced number of fat cells.

- *Age:* Though osteoporosis is not part of the normal aging process, the older individuals are the more likely that they will develop osteoporosis, because their osteoclast cells have had a longer time to thin their bones.

- *Body size:* Small, thin-boned individuals are at a greater risk than those who are heavier. Women who are obese also seem to produce more estrogen because they have so many more fat cells (though obesity may help prevent osteoporosis, it is a major risk factor for more deadly ailments such as cardiovascular disease and diabetes, so it is still not a desirable component of a healthy life; however, this is definitely an argument for not being too thin). Often people who do not build stronger bones in their growing years through exercise and proper nutrition also have a greater chance of developing osteoporosis.

- *Ethnicity:* Caucasian and Asian women

are more susceptible to osteoporosis than other nationalities. Fifty percent of Caucasian women over the age of fifty have low bone mass that will develop into osteoporosis or have had a broken bone. Only half as many African-American and Hispanic women develop osteoporosis, though nearly as many have a significant loss of bone mass.

- *Family history:* Susceptibility to bone fractures can be hereditary. People whose parents had a history of fractures tend to have reduced bone mass.

The main lifestyle risk factors are:

- Cigarette smoking
- Excessive consumption of alcohol
- General inactivity
- Steroid use (one of the main causes of

osteoporosis in children is related to steroid inhalers and oral steroids used in the treatment of asthma)

- Excessive consumption of phosphorus-laden soft drinks, especially caffeinated varieties, and coffee (caffeinated teas do not seem to have this adverse effect)
- Excessive consumption of sugar
- Excessive consumption of salt
- Excessive consumption of aluminum from various sources
- Excessive consumption of protein over an extended period of time
- Poor nutrition; especially a diet low in calcium, vitamin D, and other nutrients key to building bones

Most of the things on the second list will literally pull the calcium from your bones.

This happens because your body works hard to maintain a narrow range of calcium levels in your bloodstream. If this level drops too low, the body resorts to its vast calcium storehouse—the bones. Over time, this can result in major bone mass loss and even osteoporosis.

COMPLICATIONS OF BONE MASS LOSS

Again, the greatest complication of reduced bone mass and osteoporosis is bone fractures. These often occur when only mild stress is put on weak bones that would not otherwise break. Missing a step and falling, falling on an extended arm, or lifting a heavy object are all common events that can cause a fracture when the bone mass is low. As noted before, more than 1.5 million of these types of fractures happen annually. These can be categorized into four major groups:

- 700,000 vertebral fractures
- 300,000 hip fractures
- 250,000 wrist fractures
- 300,000 fractures in other areas

Vertebral fractures are what often cause older people to begin to "shrink" as their vertebrae weaken and then begin to gradually collapse and virtually crush one another. This loss of height is typically one of the first outward signs of osteoporosis. Of course, related back pain is another sign of the disease.

These compression fractures often crush the front of the vertebrae more than the back, causing them to take on a somewhat triangular shape and curving the spine. This condition is called *kyphosis*. When this happens, it causes the individual to walk with a stoop.

Though not half as common, hip fractures are by far the most serious complication of osteoporosis. Because these fractures often don't heal properly, one in four hip-fracture victims who could live on their own before the injury require long-term care afterward. After six months, only 15 percent of hip-fracture patients can walk across a room unaided. Another one in four dies within a year. Many of these people develop complications, such as pneumonia or blood clots, because they can no longer properly move around and care for themselves. A woman's risk of fracturing a hip is equal to her chance of developing breast, uterine, and ovarian cancer combined. Hip fractures occur two to three times more often in women than in men, yet the one-year mortality from hip fractures is roughly twice as high in men.[1]

HOW TO DETECT EARLY SIGNS OF BONE MASS REDUCTION

Since osteoporosis has no early-warning symptoms, it's very important that you check with your doctor about having your bone mass measured, especially if you are going through menopause or think you are at higher risk for the disease. This is done through a bone mineral density (BMD) test, which measures bone density in your spine, wrist, hip, heel, or hand, depending on the device used.

According to the National Institutes of

Health, BMD tests can be very effective at

- detecting low bone density before a fracture;
- confirming a diagnosis of osteoporosis if you have already experienced a fracture;
- predicting your chances of a fracture in the future;
- determining your rate of bone loss and/ or monitoring the effects of treatment if the test is conducted at intervals of a year or more.

Another subtle indicator of bone mass loss can show up in the dentist's office. Gum recession and tooth loss can be early warning signs of osteoporosis because the nutrients that keep our gums and teeth healthy are the same ones that keep our bones strong, and many of the same things that leech calcium from our bones are bad for our teeth and gums as well. If you have been to the dentist lately and discovered your gums are receding or you are in serious danger of losing a tooth, it is a good idea to see your doctor as well to have a bone mass test.

OTHER BONE DISEASES

While osteoporosis is the most common bone disease by far, it is not the only one. For our discussion in this book, we will deal with solutions and treatments for reduced bone mass and osteoporosis, but it is also informative to have a cursory understanding of some of these other bone diseases as well. Please do not assume that preventive measures outlined in this book will as effectively treat these other bone diseases as they do reduced bone mass and osteoporosis. Should you find yourself concerned with any of these other afflictions, please consult with your family physician.

PAGET'S DISEASE. In this disease, the normal process of bone breakdown and replacement happens too quickly, which can result in enlarged or deformed bones. It can be accompanied by bone pain, headaches, hearing loss, arthritis, deformities, damage to joints, and fractures. Researchers are not sure what causes Paget's disease, but one theory is that it is caused by a "slow virus" that is dormant before it starts to develop. Researchers are trying to determine whether the disease is hereditary. It rarely strikes anyone under the age of forty, and the prevalence of Paget's disease ranges from 1.5 to 8 percent depending on age and country of residence.

OSTEOGENESIS IMPERFECTA (OI). This genetic disorder causes bones to be more brittle and breakable than normal. Breaks often occur with OI for little or no apparent reason. It results when a genetic defect somehow affects the production of collagen—a protein the body uses to build connective tissues. This defect either reduces the amount of collagen available to the body or causes the collagen available to be of an inferior quality, both of which lead to weaker bones that break more easily. This disease can cause a person to have as many as several hundred fractures in a lifetime, as well as hearing loss if the structure of the ear is affected. It is estimated that between 20,000 and 50,000 individuals in the United States are affected by OI.

HYPOPHOSPHATASIA. This disorder

resembles osteogenesis imperfecta and affects one birth in 100,000. It is believed to be carried by one in 300 Americans. Depending on its severity, it can cause several problems, including the early loss of teeth, recurrent fractures, deformities, and even death. It results from low levels of an enzyme called alkaline phosphatase (ALP), which is normally present in high levels in the bones and liver. Medical science has no established therapy for hypophosphatasia.

FIBROUS DYSPLASIA. This chronic skeletal disorder causes expansion of one or more bones due to an abnormal development in the fibrous, or connective, tissue that gives infrastructure to the bones. It causes affected bones to grow unevenly and become brittle or deformed. It is a very unusual defect and generally appears in the individual before the age of ten. Recent studies seem to show that it is caused by a chemical abnormality in a bone protein that leads to the production of too much fibrous tissue in the bones affected. It is often identified after a child experiences severe pain in his bones or breaks a bone.

MYELOMA BONE DISEASE. Multiple myeloma is a malignancy of the bone marrow. In patients with myeloma, bone reabsorption exceeds bone formation. In other words, the osteoclasts, those cells that break down bones, work harder than the osteoblasts, the builders, do. Most patients with myeloma develop soft spots in their bones where the bone structure has been damaged. These occur mostly in the spine, ribs, pelvis, and skull. Myeloma not only causes pain, fractures, and hypercalcemia (excessive calcium in the blood), but also sometimes causes deformity and nerve compression problems. The incidence of myeloma is three or four in 100,000 people in the United States, and approximately 13,500 new cases are diagnosed each year. Myeloma is more common in men than in women and in African-Americans than Caucasians.

OSTEOPETROSIS. This condition is somewhat the opposite of osteoporosis. The osteoclasts do not function normally, resulting in bones that become overly dense and the cavity for bone marrow doesn't form. Thus the bones can't resist everyday stress and break easily. The congenital form of osteopetrosis afflicts between one in 100,000 and one in 500,000 infants. The adult form of this disease affects one in 20,000.

PRIMARY HYPERPARATHYROIDISM. In this

disease one or more of the parathyroid glands produces too much parathyroid hormone, causing high levels of calcium in the blood. Because of this, calcium is continually leached from the bones; more calcium is coming out of the bones than going in. The bones may be painful and break easily. Other problems may include high blood pressure and kidney stones. In the United States, twenty-eight out of 100,000 people develop primary hyperparathyroidism each year. Frequency of the disease increases with age, and women who develop the disease outnumber men three to one.

For more detailed information on any of these diseases, visit the National Institute of Health's Web site for osteoporosis and related bone diseases at *www.osteo.org*.

"NONE OF THESE DISEASES"

In Exodus 15:26, God told the Israelites that if they would listen to His voice and do what is right, He would not allow any of the diseases that the Egyptians had to come on them: "For I am the Lord that healeth thee." Bone disease is more of a concern than most of us would like to admit, but ignoring it is not the answer. By understanding it and doing a few simple things, it can be prevented. I believe that many of the recent scientific breakthroughs concerning our health are part of God's effort to reach His people with this healing message. We simply need to listen to His voice through prayer, find reliable information, and then "do what is right."

The more I have studied health concerns, the more I have found that changes that will help our bones and our health in general are often very simple to understand. I have also found that if we make basic changes, several diseases that we may face are addressed at once. For example, something as simple as adopting a healthier diet or exercising regularly can help not only our bones but also go a long way toward preventing heart disease, cancer, diabetes, and other major causes of death in the United States, not to mention improving overall quality of life. Yet even though the steps may be simple, you still have to discipline yourself to make healthy choices a part of your everyday life.

In the next chapter, we will look at some of the things God has revealed to modern science that can be done to maintain bone health and even improve it if you are already suffering from bone mass loss. It is good to know that we can combine this natural information with the power of prayer for our healing from bone disease.

Chapter 3

PREVENTING AND TREATING BONE DISEASE

Chapter 3

PREVENTING AND TREATING BONE DISEASE

Treating osteoporosis is not a simple matter and should be discussed with your health-care provider. Physicians may prescribe medications to slow or stop bone loss, increase bone density, and reduce fracture risk; however, these medications can be accompanied by side effects such as abdominal or musculoskeletal pain, nausea, heartburn, and even hot flashes. Also, estrogen replacement therapy prescribed to replace the drop in estrogen a woman experiences during menopause, while effective at preventing or treating osteoporosis, has been shown to increase a woman's risk of endometrial cancer. There's also increasing concern over recent studies indicating that women using hormone replacement therapy are at greater risk for heart disease.

Taking the steps now to prevent bone loss (or to build bone tissue if you already have some bone loss) is the key to reducing your risk of developing osteoporosis in the future. There are basically three things that you can do to help your bones stay strong and healthy:

1. Eliminate calcium robbers from your diet and habits.
2. Exercise.

3. Get proper nutrition through a healthy diet and supplements.

ELIMINATE THE BONE ROBBERS

As discussed in the previous chapter, there are several things that can leech calcium from our bones. Considering these, here are some things that you should do to reduce bone loss due to these calcium robbers:

1. **Stop smoking and/or avoid secondhand smoke.**
2. **Limit alcohol consumption.** Alcohol interferes with your body's ability to absorb calcium, making you more likely to lose bone.
3. **Avoid sweets, sugar, and junk food.** Sugar is a major culprit in

decreasing calcium levels, as it causes calcium to be pulled from your bones and eliminated out of your system. (It also increases your risk for diabetes and heart disease.) Before the twentieth century, the average American ate about ten to twelve pounds of sugar a year. Today, the average American eats about 139 pounds of sugar a year. This means that about a fifth of the calories we take in daily are from sugar, which has no nutritional value. Imagine what would happen if we consumed all of those calories from nutrient-rich foods! This step alone would go a long way toward solving the general deficiencies we face today.

4. **Limit salt consumption.** A high-

sodium diet, especially in postmenopausal women, seems to increase the amount of calcium excreted in the urine.

5. **Avoid taking any form of steroids if at all possible.** Some asthma and rheumatoid arthritis medications contain steroids, which accelerate bone loss. Ask your doctor about safer alternatives.

6. **Limit soft drinks and coffee; drink tea instead.** Soft drinks contain phosphorus, caffeine, and sugar, all of which pull calcium from the bones. Caffeine in coffee does this as well, while the caffeine in tea does not. Studies show that people who drink green or black teas not only have stronger bones, but tea also helps fight heart disease, cancer,

and Parkinson's disease.

7. **Avoid high protein consumption.**
   One of the drawbacks of the high-protein weight-loss diets that have become so popular is the damage done to our bones if we are on the diets too long. Eskimos have one of the highest levels of osteoporosis in the world, yet they take in twice as much calcium as is recommended, are outdoors a lot, and get a good deal of exercise. Why the high bone-mass loss? Diet. They eat a lot of fish, as well as whale blubber. *Too much* protein leeches calcium from the bones.

8. **Avoid aluminum intake.** If you boil water or cook food in aluminum pans, they will pick up some aluminum, which is ingested from what-

ever is cooked. Replace, when possible, your aluminum cooking
utensils and pans with those that do
not contain aluminum.

9. **Avoid unnecessary use of thyroid
   hormones.** While it was once
   believed that these would stimulate
   metabolism and help individuals
   lose weight, they have, in fact, been
   found to pull calcium from your
   bones and have little benefit for losing weight. These medications have
   been correlated to brittle bones and
   fractures.

Taking these steps is a great way to help
prevent bone-mass loss, but now let's look at
some ways we can keep our bodies *building*
bone mass.

EXERCISE STRENGTHENS YOUR BONES

Regular exercise may be the best way to keep bones strong and joints working smoothly. Bones have the unique ability to adjust their mass in response to pressure and stress. Weight-bearing exercise such as walking, jogging, dancing, jumping rope, playing tennis or basketball, backpacking, and weight lifting are particularly good for your bones. Swimming, on the other hand, is not considered a weight-bearing exercise because the water supports your body weight, though it is still a great cardiovascular exercise. Walking is one of the best exercises to keep your hips strong and keep the ball of the hip joint working smoothly within its socket. Stretching exercises are also tremendously beneficial because they also encourage the full range of motion of bones in sockets, which we lose if we don't exercise regularly.

An adequate amount of exercise can be as simple as walking for forty to forty-five minutes three to five times a week or taking a brisk walk for about thirty minutes every day. This is enough to get your heart rate up and doesn't require an expensive membership to a health club. You could exercise more, of course, but I believe it's best to start with simple changes and then work your way up as God leads you. If you're not accustomed to walking, you'll need to start with shorter walks and build up to longer walks as your fitness improves. It is important not to start with too much activity since that can stress your system more than help.

The important thing is to find something you enjoy and can do regularly that exercises and builds the aerobic capacity of your heart and lungs, as well as strengthens your bones and other body systems. As you improve your fitness, you can combine various forms of exercise to address all of the various bone and muscle groups and body systems. Remember to do proper warm-ups and cool-downs. It is also better to eat after exercising rather than before, as exercise contributes to food absorption and burning calories.

DETERMINE YOUR SAFE HEART-RATE RANGE

Whatever exercise you choose, work at it vigorously enough to get your heart rate elevated during the time you are exercising. Physical fitness experts have a simple formula for determining a safe heart-rate range for exercising. Simply subtract your age from

220 to find your maximum heart rate. If you are forty years old, your formula would be 220–40 = 180. Your target heart-rate zone is between 60 and 80 percent of that number. Multiply your maximum heart rate by 0.6 for the bottom of your safe exercise range and by 0.8 for the top. The safe heart-rate range for a forty-year-old would be between 108 and 144.

As you exercise, check your pulse rate occasionally to be sure it falls within your safe range. Find your pulse on your wrist or neck, count the number of beats in ten seconds, and multiply that number by six. If the number you get is within your safe exercise range, you're fine. If it's lower, work harder. If it's higher, slow down a little. When starting an exercise program, aim at the lowest part of your target zone for the first few

weeks. Gradually build up to the higher part
of your target zone.

Your heart rate is not crucial if you are
only interested in exercising your bones. Just
getting out and walking will do you all the
good you may need in that area.

YOUR BONES NEED LOTS OF NUTRIENTS!

While our diet is still the foundation of
good nutrition, more and more research is
showing that without supplements we cannot get everything our bodies need. The
American Medical Association, which has
traditionally taken the stand that we can get
all of the nutrients we need from our food,
has recently changed that stance because of
the mounting evidence to the contrary. For

the first time, even the medical community is telling people they need to start taking their vitamins.[1]

Yet the first, and perhaps most difficult, step is to control what we eat every day. In the previous section I gave a list of "don'ts," many of which were diet issues. Certainly you could eliminate these things from your diet to significantly increase your bone and general health, but in my more than twenty-five years of practice as a doctor of preventive medicine, I have found that it's hard for people to stick to any diet based mostly on "don'ts." The key is to replace your cravings for bad foods with cravings for good foods. You can't just eliminate things; you have to change the whole way you eat, and then this new pattern will be the basis for improved health. I have yet to find a better way to do this than by encouraging people to adapt to something closer to the Mediterranean diet.

THE MEDITERRANEAN DIET

Recent articles appearing in *Scientific American* and *Newsweek* have cited the switch from the old Food Guide Pyramid (breads and cereals as the base, fruits and vegetables on the next level, then dairy two or three times a day, two or three servings a day of meat and proteins, and topped with fats, oils, and sweets used sparingly) to a new food pyramid that looks surprising like the Mediterranean diet we have been recommending in our ministry for some time. This new pyramid has daily exercise and weight control at its base; whole-grain foods and plant oils—olive, canola, etc.—at the next level (suggesting these are eaten at most meals); followed by fruits and vegetables (five to nine servings a day); nuts and legumes or beans (one to three servings a day); fish, poultry, and eggs (zero to two servings a day); dairy or calcium supplement (once or twice a day); and red meat, butter, white rice, white bread, potatoes, pasta, and sweets at the top (eaten sparingly).[2] This switch in the food pyramid is just part of the new emphasis on nutrition for prevention that is happening in the medical community. Such a diet is not only healthy for your bones, but it's also healthy for your cardiovascular, immune, digestive, and other systems.

Another advantage of such a diet is that it has many natural compounds that can act as estrogen replacers for women going through menopause—the time when most women begin to lose bone mass at the fastest rate. Plant-derived estrogens, called phyto-estrogens, can be obtained from the flava-nones in citrus fruit; the isoflavones in leg-umes such as chick-peas, soy, lentils, red clover, and beans; the flavonols and flavones found in red and yellow fruits and vegeta-bles; and the lignans (which also stop the breakdown of bone and replenish bone structure) found in flaxseed and certain cere-als. This explains why Asian women, whose diets are high in these substances, suffer from neither the symptoms of menopause nor have the breast cancer risk associated with many estrogen-replacement drugs. So, again, by eating a varied, healthy diet you address many issues at once: menopause, cancer, and bone health!

If you were to look at the typical menus of families living in the Mediterranean countries, you would see that the following items make up the bulk of what is eaten every day:

- **Olive oil.** Olive oil replaces most fats, oils, butter, and margarine. Extra-virgin olive oil is preferred over other varieties.
- **Breads.** Dark, chewy, high-fiber crusty bread is present at most meals in the Mediterranean. Another good choice is Ezekiel bread, a recipe based on Ezekiel 4:9. (The typical American white bread made from processed white flours is not part of this diet.) Such refined-grain breads lose a significant amount of nutrients in the production process. For example, when whole wheat is refined into white flour, it loses 72 percent of its vitamin B_6, 67 percent of its folic acid, 60 percent of its calcium, 85 percent of

its magnesium, 86 percent of its manganese, 68 percent of its copper, and 78 percent of its zinc.[3] Since grains and breads make up about 30 percent of our diet, we can quite significantly increase our overall vitamin and mineral intake if we consume whole foods instead of processed foods.

- **Pasta, rice, couscous, bulgur, and potatoes.** Pasta is often served with fresh vegetables and herbs sautéed in olive oil; occasionally it is served with small quantities of lean beef. Tomato sauces, often served with pasta, are high in lycopene, which is one of the most potent antioxidants (substances that absorb or neutralize harmful free radicals). Brown rice is preferred. Couscous and bulgur are other forms of whole grains.

- **Grains.** The Mediterranean diet includes healthy grains from a variety of sources. One of the easiest ways for Americans to get grains into their diet is by eating cereals containing wheat bran (one-half cup, four to five times a week), or alternating wheat bran with cereals such as Bran Buds (one-half cup) or with cereals containing oat bran (one-third cup). Eating cereal with soy milk rather than regular milk adds extra benefits because soy is a whole protein and a great source of phytoestrogens. (For more information on soy, see the next section.)

- **Fruits.** A variety of fruits are available in the Mediterranean region, and they are usually eaten raw and at least two or three times a day. These are a great replacement for sugary snacks and junk food. Consuming five dried plums a day (what used to "unfashionably" be called prunes) can actually restore bone mass back to normal because of the bone-mineral protecting compounds in them.

- **Beans.** Include various kinds of beans in your diet: pinto, great northern, navy, kidney, and lentils. Bean and lentil soups are very popular in the Mediterranean countries and are usually prepared with a small amount of olive oil. It is good to eat at least one-half cup of beans three or four times weekly.

- **Nuts.** Nuts have wonderful benefits. Almonds, in particular, are higher in dietary fiber than most nuts. Ten unsalted almonds or walnuts a day is a good number.

- **Vegetables and herbs.** Dark green vegetables are prominent in the Mediterranean diet, especially in salads. The updated food pyramid suggests vegetables should be eaten daily "in abundance." It's a good idea to eat at least one of the following cruciferous vegetables daily (many of which are calcium rich): cabbage, broccoli, cauliflower, turnip greens, mustard greens. It is also wise to include at least one from the following group of fruits and vegetables daily: carrots, spinach, sweet potatoes, cantaloupe, peaches, or apricots.

- **Yogurt.** Eating fat-free live-culture yogurt daily has some incredible benefits. The live bacteria in yogurt (lactobacillus, streptococcus, and acidophilus) significantly strengthen the immune system,

which is good for all of our body
systems, including the cardiovascular.
(Unfortunately, freezing yogurt kills
these good bacteria.) Yogurt is also a
good source of calcium. A light breakfast
of one cup of fat-free yogurt with ten
almonds and chopped fruit is a great
start to the day. Eating yogurt with your
morning nutritional supplements also
reduces the "vitamin taste" that often
lingers after taking tablets and capsules
alone.

- **Cheese.** The Mediterranean diet
includes lighter colored or white cheeses,
including goat cheese, and is usually
grated or crumbled on salads or served in
small wedges along with fruit as a des-
sert. Recent studies indicate that cheese,
unlike other milk products, might not

contribute to clogged arteries as much as was previously believed. Still, it is wise to eat reduced-fat or low-fat cheeses (fat-free cheeses are typically rubbery and not very palatable).

While all of the above-mentioned should be eaten daily, meat, fish, and eggs, on the other hand, should only be eaten a few times a week. I would put these in the following order of frequency and importance:

- **Fish.** Fish is the healthiest of meats, but it still should not be consumed every day. Cod, salmon, mackerel, and herring are high on the list of desired fish, as they are high in omega-3 fatty acids (which improve calcium metabolism, especially when combined with evening primrose oil). They are also high in vitamin D, which helps calcium absorption. Trout is also a good choice.

- **Poultry.** White breast meat without the skin is best. Poultry can be eaten two or three times a week.

- **Eggs.** Eggs should be eaten no more than two or three times a week.

- **Red meat.** The fat in red meat is the least desirable of all. When God said, "You shall eat no fat," in Leviticus 7:23 RSV, I believe this is the type of fat He was referring to. Red meat eaten in Mediterranean countries tends to be much leaner and is eaten only two or three times a month. If you do include red meat in a meal, eat small portions of lean cuts and trim off the fat before you cook it.

THE SOYBEAN: NATURE'S BEST MEAT
SUBSTITUTE.

According to recent research reported in the *American Journal of Clinical Nutrition*, soy helps prevent bone loss.[4] Prescription estrogen treatments, used for several years, also help prevent bone loss and decrease osteoporosis in postmenopausal women, but these medications have potentially significant side effects and health risks. In fact, in July 2002, the Women's Health Initiative, a large federal study on the risks and benefits of hormone replacement therapy (HRT), abruptly halted one arm of the experiment five years into the scheduled eight-year term. Why? Researchers concluded that the overall health risks from HRT substantially exceeded its benefits. Originally designed to discover whether taking a combination of synthetic estrogens and progestins could lower the risk of heart disease in postmenopausal women, the study found that HRT increased the number of heart attacks in the study participants.

Risks for breast cancer, stroke, and blood clots were also substantially increased. According to data from the study, for every 10,000 women taking HRT for one year, seven more will have heart attacks than the same number of women not taking HRT. Eight more will have invasive breast cancer, and eight more will have strokes. While those numbers may sound small, they become very large when applied to the six million women estimated to be taking HRT.

Soy is a great source of phytoestrogen (in the form of isoflavones) and thus can do the same thing as estrogen therapy—prevent bone loss and decrease osteoporosis—but without the health risks. The study reported in the *American Journal of Clinical Nutrition* followed almost seventy perimenopausal women in a double-blind test where the experiment groups received foods made with isoflavone-containing soy proteins. Researchers measured the women's bone-mineral density and bone-mineral content at the beginning and at the end of the twenty-four-week study. The control group, which did not receive any of the soy products, actually showed a decrease in bone-mineral density. The groups consuming soy showed no losses.[5]

While research is continuing on the benefits of soy in multiple areas of the body, I recommend supplementation with isoflavones in soy extracts. These can protect your

cardiovascular system by lowering your cholesterol levels and even protect your bones.
While such supplements are particularly
important for women, men cannot afford to
overlook the benefits of soy. Though osteoporosis occurs less often in men, it is still a
risk, and soy foods are one way of reducing
that risk as well as that of heart disease.

NUTRITIONAL SUPPLEMENTS FOR BONE HEALTH

While diet is the foundation of nutrition,
it is next to impossible to get enough of
these key nutrients through diet alone. As a
result, it is important to make a high-quality
nutritional supplement, balanced with all the
key ingredients, an integral part of a complete program to keep your bones healthy
and strong. The following minerals, vita-

mins, and other compounds are crucial to keeping your bones strong:

CALCIUM. Although calcium still tops the list of ingredients we need to build strong bones, research has shown that the traditional advice to simply "throw calcium" at our bones will not improve bone mass if other key nutrients are not also present. Calcium cannot add itself to our bones if there is not an established framework of collagen connective tissue and protein for the calcium to attach itself to. To build this framework, we need vitamin C, vitamin D, vitamin K, magnesium, copper, and zinc. If these are not present to help build this framework, the calcium simply passes from our system, with little or no benefit to our bones.

All calcium tablets are not created equal.

The four major types of calcium available are:

- calcium hydroxyapatite
- calcium ascorbate
- calcium citrate
- calcium carbonate

Of these, calcium carbonate is perhaps the most common and the least beneficial overall. It is the form of calcium found in antacids like Tums. One of the most faddish things currently on the health food/supplement market is coral calcium, which is advertised to have special qualities over other types of calcium. However, it is the same calcium carbonate that is found in antacids. The fact that this calcium acts as an antacid is its major drawback. As we get older, our stomach tends to produce less stomach acid, so taking anything that would reduce that acid even further is ill advised. If you are taking Tums or something similar to get your calcium, you are not truly benefiting from it as much as you are reducing the amount of stomach acid you need to help digestion. Nor are you retaining this calcium, because antacids don't have the other nutrients required to build the infrastructure onto which the calcium can attach itself. Small doses can still be somewhat beneficial, so if you do take calcium in this form, make sure the small dose is combined with other forms of calcium.

Of the other forms, calcium hydroxyapatite is the best since it does not neutralize stomach acids and is closest to the type that is actually deposited into our bones. The ascorbate and citrate forms are also good, and some studies even suggest that they are easier for the body to absorb.

The average American consumes only about 600 milligrams of calcium a day. In contrast, the National Academy of Sciences recommends 1,000 milligrams a day for adults under age fifty and 1,200 milligrams for those over fifty (menopausal women may need as much as 1,500 milligrams).

VITAMIN D. This nutrient has long been recognized as crucial for proper absorption of calcium. Research suggests that it also helps immune-system function and may reduce the risk of colon cancer. Even though our bodies can make a certain amount of vitamin D when our skin is exposed to sunlight (research suggests that as little as fifteen minutes a day of sunshine can give us much of the vitamin D we need), many people spend too much time indoors or deliberately avoid the sun for fear of increasing their risk of skin cancer. Few foods contain significant amounts of this nutrient, though fatty fish, eggs, and fortified foods, such as milk, are good sources. On the other hand, many people also avoid these foods because of concerns about high fat and cholesterol. As a result, many Americans are significantly deficient in vitamin D; according to a recent study, nearly 60 percent of American adults have inadequate levels of vitamin D in their blood.

To further complicate matters, research has shown that there is an age-related decline in the body's ability to both absorb and activate vitamin D. This means that as we get older, the likelihood of becoming deficient in vitamin D increases. But this is exactly when we need vitamin D the most to help prevent bone fractures, keep our immune system functioning properly, and prevent diseases such as colon cancer. The only way to ensure that we don't fall short of this essential nutrient is to supplement our diet with a high-quality multivitamin-and-mineral product that contains an ample amount of vitamin D.

Studies have shown that women with severe osteoporosis are also low on vitamin D, but that vitamin D alone, just as calcium alone, does not help prevent bone loss. Both are needed in the prevention of bone-density reduction.

I suggest 400 to 1,200 IU (international units) a day of vitamin D_3 for strengthening or maintaining strong bones.

MAGNESIUM. Sixty percent of the U.S. population is deficient in this essential partner mineral to calcium. When the body is low in magnesium, it pulls calcium from the bones and tries to replace the needed magnesium with calcium, depositing it in various soft tissues or in artery walls, where it does more harm than good. The resulting low magnesium levels contribute to hardening of the arteries. Magnesium has been called "nature's calcium channel blocker" because it also blocks calcium from being deposited in the muscles and heart cells. Some researchers believe that magnesium is as important as calcium for proper bone health. Most of us should get at least 400 milligrams of this vital mineral daily. Those concerned more specifically with their bone health should get 750 milligrams a day.

SILICON. This trace mineral is important to

the formation of bones, hair, skin, and nails.
It appears to play an important role in making and maintaining connective tissue. Good
dietary sources of silicon are whole-grain
breads and cereals and root vegetables. I recommend 5 milligrams a day of silicon to
improve bone density.

VITAMIN C. This antioxidant vitamin is
crucial for the formation of collagen, the
bone-strengthening protein that builds the
infrastructure to which calcium attaches in
order to build bone. I recommend 2,000
milligrams of vitamin C daily for everyone
and 2,200 for those specifically concerned
with improving bone density.

VITAMIN K (PHYLLOQUINONE). This
essential vitamin is needed for the activation
of osteocalcin, a protein found in bone that

attracts calcium and allows crystal formation of the bone to occur. I recommend 400 micrograms of vitamin K a day for those wanting to increase bone mass.

BORON. This nonmetallic element increases estrogen levels and increases bone density. It appears to improve the metabolism of calcium, magnesium, copper, and vitamin D in the body, thus also reducing their loss. It is found in such foods as raisins, dried plums (prunes), and nuts—and to a slightly lesser extent in non-citrus fruits, legumes, and other vegetables. I recommend taking 5 milligrams of boron per day.

ZINC. This mineral is essential for normal bone-cell formation as well as for the synthesis of various proteins found in bone tissue. I recommend 15 milligrams of zinc a day for everyone and an additional 7.5 milligrams daily for those concerned with improving bone health.

COPPER. This trace mineral is crucial to the synthesis of the collagen component of bone tissue. I recommend 2 milligrams of copper daily for everyone and those who want to improve their bone density should take 3 milligrams a day.

MANGANESE. This mineral is also critical for building the bone matrix that holds calcium in place and builds bones. A new interest in the effect of manganese on bone health began when famed Portland Trailblazer Bill Walton's repeated ankle fractures were halted with manganese supplementation. The best sources of manganese are whole grains, avocados, grape juice, chocolate, legumes, nuts, egg yolks, seeds, boysenberries, blueberries, pineapple, spinach, collard greens, seaweed, peas, and other green vegetables. All of us should have 7.5 milligrams of manganese daily and those concerned with building bones should have 10 milligrams a day.

ISOFLAVONE COMPLEX. As previously discussed, these natural phytoestrogenic compounds derived from soy, red clover, fo-ti (a root herb), and hops promote bone health. They also help regulate hormone balance and support the cardiovascular system. I recommend 30 milligrams a day of a good isoflavone complex for all who want to improve their bone density.

USEFUL HERBS. Dong quai (Angelica sinensis root) has been used clinically for decades in Asia to treat menopause and reduce the complications associated with osteoporosis. This herb contains phytoestrogens for estrogen replacement just as the isoflavones do. In a Japanese study, menopausal women who were treated with an herbal formula containing dong quai and vitamin D_3 showed a 5 to 7 percent increase in bone-mineral content.

Other herbs that support calcium metabolism include horsetail, oatstraw, and nettle. All are rich in calcium and other trace minerals.

PRESCRIPTION MEDICATIONS FOR OSTEOPOROSIS

Most prescription medications for the treatment of osteoporosis—the most common being Fosomax—work by inhibiting the bone deconstructing action of the osteo-clast cells. This group of medications is called bisphosphonates. The main drawbacks are that drugs in this class can cause esophageal problems and are very expensive. When taken as directed, patients must drink a full glass of water and sit upright for a full thirty minutes after taking the drugs. This is to make sure that the drug stays in the stomach until it is digested. Otherwise, a condition called erosive esophagitis can occur.

However, God has given us a natural alternative that comes from the hops plant and has no such side effects. It is called Osteogene. Quite a bit of research has been done in Japan on this extract. It has a chemical in it called humulone that stops bone from being reabsorbed in the same way Fosomax does, but without the threat to the esophagus or acid reflux. Osteogene also appears to act as a COX–2 inhibitor, and there is some evidence that it can reduce the risk of some forms of cancer as well as reduce the size of tumors. I include 10 milligrams of Osteogene in my daily bone support supplements.

A SAFETY CHECKLIST TO PREVENT FALLS

Each year, about one-third of adults aged sixty-five and older experience falls that can result in broken bones and other injuries. Avoiding such falls can go a long way toward reducing the risk of complications from bone mass loss. In many cases, these falls could be prevented by taking some simple steps to eliminate common household hazards. Look around your house and take these precautions so that you or a loved one doesn't fall.

- **Floors:** Remove all loose wires and cords; minimize clutter. If you have throw rugs, either remove them or make sure they are smooth and anchored with slip-proof material underneath. Try to keep furniture in the same place.
- **Bathrooms:** Install grab bars and nonskid tape in the tub or shower.
- **Lighting:** Make sure halls, stairways, and entrances are well lit. Install nightlights, especially in bathrooms, and always turn a light on before you get up in the middle of the night.
- **Kitchen:** Install nonskid rubber mats near the sink and stove. Be sure to clean

up spills immediately.

- **Stairs:** Make sure treads, rails, and rugs are secure and that carpets are smooth with no bumps or bulges that can cause tripping.
- **Shoes:** Wear sturdy rubber-soled shoes.
- **Be aware of the side effects of medications.** Read the labels of your prescription drugs. Many prescription drugs may make you dizzy or light-headed. Others may affect your vision, hearing, muscle strength, coordination, reflexes, or balance. If your medications list these possible side effects, go the extra mile to avoid an accident or check with your physician to see if there is another alternative to this medication.

GOD WILL GIVE STRENGTH
TO YOUR BONES

Despite what medical science may say, God can give strength and healing to feeble bones just as He did when Peter called on the name of Jesus for the healing of the lame man at the temple gate. The situation may look impossible, but with God all things are possible. We need to do what we can, and if we will hear and obey His voice, God will do His part.

In John 10:10, Jesus told us that He came that we might have life and that we might have it more abundantly. In Psalm 91:16, God told us He would satisfy us with long life and show us His salvation. Being stooped or crippled by osteoporosis or bone mass loss is not part of an abundant and satisfying life. Prayerfully consider this information and follow the steps in the next chapter so that God can lead you on the pathway to healing bone disease that He has for you.

Chapter 4

YOUR DAILY WALK ON THE PATHWAY TO HEALTHY BONES

Chapter 4

YOUR DAILY WALK ON THE PATHWAY TO HEALTHY BONES

> Ye shall serve the Lord your God, and he shall bless thy bread, and thy water; and *I will take sickness away from the midst of thee*. There shall nothing cast their young, nor be barren, in thy land: *the number of thy days I will fulfill*. (Exodus 23:25–26, emphasis author's)

This passage of Scripture has always been a central one to our ministry, as in it

God so clearly links His blessings of health to our bread and water—symbolic of the things we eat and drink. This is especially relevant to our discussion of bone health because it is also so dependent on our diet. Even early Greek medical doctors picked up on this fact. Hippocrates, author of the Hippocratic oath, which is still used today as the ethic standard for the practice of medicine, said, "Let your food be your medicine and let your medicine be your food."

Notice in our Scripture that God also ties the blessing of our food with service to Him. I have always believed that serving God is not only ministry, as many immediately think when they hear the words *serving God,* but also includes walking every day according to His guidance and direction. Certainly we serve Him by active involvement in our churches, but we also serve Him by obeying His Word in how we conduct ourselves in our places of employment, in our social lives, in nurturing our families, and in taking care of ourselves. As the Scriptures say:

> Don't you know that you yourselves [your bodies] are God's temple and that God's Spirit lives in you? If anyone destroys God's temple [your bodies], God will destroy him; for God's temple is sacred, and you [your bodies] are that temple. (1 Corinthians 3:16–17 NIV, bracketed words are author's)

God clearly wants us to take care of ourselves so that we can live long, full lives as lights for Him on this earth.

I also believe we see the pattern of how

God wants us to operate in our lives—by combining spiritual principles with natural wisdom. There are five steps for developing this combination of spiritual and physical well-being in our lives. They outline how we can find either His plan for healthy living (if we are maintaining our health and avoiding disease) or His pathway to healing whatever health challenges we or our loved ones may be facing today.

Step 1: Consult with a physician or reliable medical professional. Be sure to have regular checkups to catch potential problems early, when they are easiest to treat and correct. Many people say they don't need to go to doctors because they are doing all the things they need to do in order to maintain their health. I believe we need to do both: live healthy lifestyles and see our doctors regularly. One need not exclude the other. Having a checkup when you're feeling healthy can keep you from unnecessary worry about your health. Since osteoporosis is a silent disease until it results in a fracture, regular checkups and bone density tests are the best ways to catch it early enough to prevent it. Regular checkups also give you a chance to discuss with your doctor your plans for maintaining or regaining your health.

Consultation with a physician or a competent medical professional actually gives you something that books such as this one cannot—insight into solutions or maintenance plans that specifically fit your unique medical and physical needs. Be sure also to discuss with your health advisor all of the various compounds and medications you are taking to ensure that there are no conflicts.

This person may even be able to suggest a packaged supplement program that contains all or most of what you need to take on a daily basis, making nutritional supplementation even easier. Discuss your diet and exercise programs with your doctor to see if he or she has any other advice that might be helpful to you in these areas. This first step is crucial to finding the pathway that is unique for you.

Step 2: Pray with understanding. Seek God in prayer and ask Him to reveal to you and to your doctor the best steps in the natural to proceed down your pathway to maintaining your health or receiving your healing.

While much of the advice offered in this book is directed at your body, it's equally important that you do not neglect your daily spiritual needs. Make sure to "supplement" what you take into your mind and body every day with solid doses of God's Word and prayer—avoiding those things that are harmful to your spirit in the same way that you avoid junk foods or other things that are harmful to your "temple." Only then can God lead you into the fullness and abundance of life He has promised you in all areas.

If you are not sure how to pray for bone health, you might begin by praying a prayer like the following one, and then adapt it as the Spirit of God leads you in order to make it fit the specific concerns and needs you want to address in prayer:

> Father, I thank you, in the name of
> Jesus, that you are able by your power
> to strengthen my bones, just as you did

for the man in Acts chapter 3.

I also thank you, Father, for helping me do the right things in the natural to prevent osteoporosis and bone mass loss and that you will guide me down the path to doing what I can to strengthen my bones. Give me the self-discipline to change my diet so that I eat more bone-building foods and avoid those things that will leech calcium from my bones. Help me find an exercise program that I enjoy so I will make it a part of my weekly routine. Guide me to finding the right nutritional supplements to take regularly, and help me develop the self-control to remember to take them every day.

Also reveal to me the medications or natural alternatives that are best for me to defeat bone disease. I pray that your healing anointing will flow through these substances and that if I need to take pharmaceutical medications it will be for as short a time as possible as more natural compounds take their place. However you lead me, I will be obedient to the guidance of your Holy Spirit.

Thank you, Father, for setting me free from sickness and disease as you bless what I eat and drink, and thank you that I will fulfill the number of my days according to your promises.

In Jesus' name, I thank you for your answer. Amen.

Step 3: Ask the Holy Spirit to guide you to the truth. I have given you a great deal of information about things you can do, eat, or take to help your body control and defeat bone mass loss, and it is quite possible that your medical advisor will give you some other options. By referring to the information in this book, you can ask your health professional what would be best specifically for you. Ask her if she would be willing to work with you in developing a diet and exercise program or nutritional supplement program or if she can suggest other steps for you to keep osteoporosis and fractures from being a problem for you.

I strongly encourage you to explore all the aspects of the information I have shared with you in this book. Then pray in faith that God will give you the wisdom you need in order to discern the pathway He has provided that is best for you. In James 1:5 we have God's promise about receiving this wisdom: "If any of you lack wisdom, let him ask of God, that giveth to all men liberally, and upbraideth not; and it shall be given him." Jesus also told us, "But when he, the Spirit of truth [the Holy Spirit], comes, he will guide you into all truth" (John 16:13 NIV, bracketed words are author's). Allow the Holy Spirit to guide you to *all* truth, even that concerning the proper care of your physical body.

Step 4: Maintain healthy nutrition. Exercise your body and mind to stay fit. In other words, dedicate yourself to living a bone-strengthening lifestyle. Make the dietary changes outlined in this book, taking the proper supplements, and an excercise program, all a regular part of your routine—and remember to make them fun and not a burden. Find a variety of foods and recipes consistent with the Mediterranean diet, and that you like, and experiment with these healthy natural ingredients to create your own delicious meals. Find an exercise program you enjoy. While some people like walking on a treadmill while watching television, others need to get outside or find a competitive sport to challenge them; some people prefer a group activity, such as dance or stretching classes to encourage them socially, as well.

Studies have shown that we also need to challenge ourselves intellectually to maintain healthier mental faculties. Read, play games, and study subjects that interest you so that you continue to grow intellectually no matter what your age. Establish an active life for an active body and mind.

Step 5: Stand firm in God's pathway to healing for you. Refuse to be discouraged or defeated. Be aggressive in prayer and in faith, claiming your health and healing in Jesus Christ. And when God compels you to make a lifestyle change as the result of something you have learned from a reliable source, put it into action.

GOD HAS A UNIQUE PATHWAY TO HEALTH FOR YOU

There are nineteen individually recorded healings in the Gospels, and each is unique in its own way. I believe these are all recorded in the Scriptures to show us that God uses different pathways to deliver His healing power. When I realized this, it totally changed the way I practiced medicine. It is amazing to me how when I started praying and asking God to show me, as a doctor, His pathway to healing for each of my patients, I began to see more and more clearly His design for helping each person. Through prayer, faith, knowledge, and wisdom, God can show you His pathway to maintaining health or receiving healing.

If we are simply open to that, God will work miracles. It may be instantaneous, or it may be a process or treatment that takes some time. Just as many chronic diseases, such as osteoporosis, diabetes, and cardiovascular disease take some time to develop, they also take some time to be reversed. It may involve certain prescription medications for a time, or even surgery. Or it may be a pathway that is relatively uneventful as we have regular checkups and maintain our health. Thank God that we can pray for our healing, but let us also be thankful that we can take precautions before we are sick to avoid the need for healing. Either way, as Christians we have tremendous hope.

Hebrews 11:1 says that faith gives substance to those things we hope for. If you don't have anything to hope for, how will your faith give substance to it? You have to have hope, and that hope comes when you know that God has a pathway to health or healing for you. That is a promise you can hold on to, pray for, and have faith in. Thank God for His promises!

These are principles you can apply in all areas of your life, but they can be specifically applied with regard to your physical health. See a physician for the information you will need in order to know how to pray, and then seek God in the areas where you have a health concern. God knows your needs and the best way for you to receive your healing and maintain your health. Hold on to the hope of His promises and He will show you His plan for healthy living that is designed especially for you.

ENDNOTES

Introduction

1. National Osteoporosis Foundation Web site, "Disease Statistics": *www.nof.org/osteoporosis/ stats.htm*.
2. National Osteoporosis Foundation Web site, "America's Bone Health: The State of Osteoporosis and Low Bone Mass": *www.nof.org/ advocacy/prevalence/index.htm*.

Chapter 2

1. National Osteoporosis Foundation Web site, "Disease Statistics."

Chapter 3

1. Robert H. Fletcher, M.D., M.S.; and Kathleen M. Fairfield, M.D., D.P.H.; "Vitamins

for Chronic Disease Prevention in Adults: Clinical Applications," *The Journal of the American Medical Association* 287, no. 23 (19 June 2002): 3129.

2. Walter C. Willet and Meir J. Stampfer, "Rebuilding the Food Pyramid," *Scientific American* 228, no. 1 (January 2003): 64–71; and Geoffrey Cowley, "A Better Way to Eat," *Newsweek* 141, no. 3 (20 January 2003): 46–54.

3. H. A. Schroeder, "Losses of Vitamins and Trace Minerals Resulting From Processing and Preservation of Foods," *American Journal of Clinical Nutrition* 24, no. 5 (May 1971): 562–73.

4. D. L. Alekel, et al., "Isoflavone-Rich Soy Protein Isolate Attenuates Bone Loss in the Lumbar Spine of Perimenopausal Women," *American Journal of Clinical Nutrition* Vol. 72, no. 3 (September 2000): 844–52.

5. Ibid.

REGINALD B. CHERRY, M.D.—A MEDICAL DOCTOR'S TESTIMONY

The first six years of my life were lived in the dusty rural town of Mansfield, in the Ouachita Mountains of western Arkansas. In those childhood years, I had one seemingly impossible dream—to become a doctor!

Through God's grace, I graduated from Baylor University and the University of Texas Medical School. Throughout those years, I felt God tug on my heart a number of times, especially through Billy Graham as I heard him preach on television. But I never surrendered my life to Jesus Christ.

In those early days of practicing medicine, I met Dr. Kenneth Cooper and became trained in the field of preventive medicine. In the mid-seventies I moved to Houston and established a medical practice for preventive medicine. I am sad to say that at that time money became a driving force in my life.

Nevertheless, God is good. He brought into our clinic a nurse who became a Spirit-filled Christian, and she began praying for me. In fact, she had her whole church praying for me!

In my search for fulfillment and meaning in life, I called out to God one night in late November 1979, and prayed, "Jesus, I give you everything I own. I'm sorry for the life I've lived. I want to live for you the rest of my days. I give you my life." A doctor was born again. And that beautiful nurse, Linda, who had prayed for me and shared Jesus with me, is now my wife!

Not only did Jesus transform my life but He also transformed my medical practice. God spoke to me and said in effect, "I want you to establish a Christian clinic. From now on when you practice medicine, you will be *ministering* to patients." I began to pray for patients seeking God's pathway to healing in the supernatural realm as well as in the natural realm.

Over the years we have witnessed how God has miraculously used both supernatural and natural pathways to heal our patients and to demonstrate His marvelous healing and saving power.

I know what God has done in my life, and I know what God has done in the lives of our patients. He can do the same in yours—He has a unique pathway to healing for you! He is the Lord that heals you (see Exodus 15:26). By His stripes you were healed (see Isaiah 53:5).

Linda and I stand with you as you seek God's unique pathway for you to healthy bones.

If you do not know Jesus Christ as your personal Lord and Savior, I invite you to pray this prayer and ask Jesus into your life:

Lord Jesus, I invite you into my life as my Lord and Savior. I repent of my past sins. I ask you to forgive me. Thank you for shedding your blood on the cross to cleanse me from my sin and to heal me. I receive your gift of everlasting life and I surrender all to you. Thank you, Jesus, for saving me. Amen.

ABOUT THE AUTHOR

Reginald B. Cherry, M.D., did his pre-med at Baylor University, graduated from the University of Texas Medical School, and has practiced diagnostic and preventive medicine for more than twenty-five years. His work in medicine was recognized and honored by the city of Houston and by President George W. Bush when he was governor of Texas.

Dr. Cherry and his wife, Linda, a clinical nurse who has worked with Dr. Cherry and his patients during the past two-and-a-half decades, now host the popular television program *The Doctor and the Word*, which has a potential viewing audience of 90 million homes weekly. They also publish a monthly medical newsletter and produce topical audiocassette teachings, pocket books, and booklets. Dr. Cherry is author of the bestselling books *The Doctor and the Word*, *The Bible Cure*, and *Healing Prayer*.

RESOURCES AVAILABLE FROM REGINALD B. CHERRY MINISTRIES, INC.

Prayers That Heal: Faith-Building Prayers When You Need a Miracle

Combining the wisdom of over twenty-five years of medical practice and the revelation of God's Word, Dr. Cherry provides the knowledge you need to pray effectively against diabetes, cancer, heart disease, eye problems, hypoglycemia, and fifteen other common afflictions that rob you of your health.

Healing Prayer

A fascinating in-depth look at a vital link between spiritual and physical healing. Dr. Cherry presents actual case histories of people who were healed through prayer, plus the latest information on herbs, vitamins, and supplements that promote vibrant health. This is sound information you will need to keep you healthy—mind, soul, and body.

God's Pathway to Healing: Diabetes

Diabetes is reaching epidemic propor-tions as 17 million Americans now face the disease and another one million a year will develop it. Some statistics suggest that by the year 2025, one in four Americans will have diabetes. The severe complications of diabetes also give us pause for concern in that it more than triples the risk of death for young adults who acquire it. However, God has a pathway both for prevention and healing of this proliferating disease. In this book, Dr. Cherry outlines the lifestyle changes to prevent and control diabetes and discusses the best medications and natural alternatives for reducing its threat to our overall health.

God's Pathway to Healing: Digestion

Dr. Cherry discusses keys to a naturally healthy digestive system, including better digestion and absorption of food, proper elimination of waste, and the place of "good" bacteria. He points readers toward better eating habits and natural nutritional supplements to improve digestion.

God's Pathway to Healing: Heart

Heart disease kills twice as many people as all of the different forms of cancer combined, and more than half of the Christian community dies of coronary artery or cardiovascular diseases. However, there are things you can do to keep free of heart disease. An incredible wealth of research in recent years has been done on natural extracts and foods that will feed the heart muscle and keep it strong and healthy. When these nutrients are combined with faith, prayer, and God's Word, you will quickly find yourself on God's pathway to healing and a healthy heart.

God's Pathway to Healing: Herbs That Heal

Learn the truth about common herbal remedies and discover the possible side effects of each. Discover which herbs can help treat symptoms of insomnia, arthritis, heart problems, asthma, and many other conditions. This pocket book will help you determine whether herbs are part of God's pathway to healing for you.

God's Pathway to Healing: The Immune System

We truly are fearfully and wonderfully made, and part of that amazing creation is the structure God put into humanity to keep us all healthy for life: our immune system! In this insightful pocket book, Dr. Cherry explains the basic function of this everyday miracle that even medical science has yet to fully understand and steps we can take to keep it strong and balanced so that it will do what God designed it to do: take sickness away from our midst (see Exodus 23:25).

God's Pathway to Healing: Joints and Arthritis

Painful joints and arthritis do not have to be part of aging, says Dr. Cherry. Recent medical breakthroughs show that natural substances can relieve pain and inflammation and slow or prevent cartilage loss.

God's Pathway to Healing: Memory and Mental Acuity

As the baby-boomer generation ages, we are facing more problems with mental function than ever before. In this pocket book, Dr. Cherry addresses concerns about depression, attention deficit hyperactivity disorder (ADHD), migraine headaches, Alzheimer's disease, and many other problems that we associate with the brain's function. Whether it is because of age-related memory loss, poor nutrition, or the pollutants we take in daily, people of all ages need new information about how to keep their minds healthy and strong.

God's Pathway to Healing: Menopause

This book is full of helpful advice for women who are going through what can be a very stressful time of life. Find out which foods, supplements, and steps lead to a pathway to healing for menopause and perimenopause.

God's Pathway to Healing: Prostate

This little book is packed with enlightening insights for men who are searching for ways to prevent prostate cancer or who have actually been diagnosed with the disease. Discover how foods, plant-derived natural supplements, and a change in diet can be incorporated into your life to help you find a pathway to healing for prostate disease.

God's Pathway to Healing: Vision

Macular degeneration, cataracts, vision degeneration due to complications of diabetes, and other eye conditions can be slowed or prevented. Dr. Cherry discusses herbs and nutritional changes people can make to keep their vision strong.

God's Pathway to Healing: Vitamins and Supplements

With the huge number of supplements and multivitamins on the market today, it is often difficult to know what to take to get what we need and what not to take to make sure we don't get amounts that might be harmful to our systems. In this age where new and epidemic diseases seem to be discovered more regularly than ever before, this pocket book could well be the key you need to discovering the miraculous power God has unlocked through natural extracts and nutritional supplements to keep you healthy and whole to the end of your days on earth.

Dr. Cherry's Little Instruction Book for Health and Healing

Easy-to-read information about healthy habits, natural remedies, and nutritional guidance along with biblical principles for supernatural healing, prayers, and Scripture make this a great reminder that God's desire is that His people be healthy. This is a helpful small volume for readers familiar with Dr. Cherry's work and a great introduction for those who are new to his ministry.

The Bible Cure (now in paperback)

Dr. Cherry presents the hidden truths in the Bible taken from ancient dietary health laws, describes how Jesus anointed with natural substances to heal, and explains how to activate faith through prayer for health and healing. This book validates scientific medical research by comparing it to God's original health plan.

The Doctor and the Word (now in paperback)

Dr. Cherry introduces how God has a pathway to healing for you. Jesus sometimes healed instantaneously and supernaturally, while other healings involved a process. Discover how the manifestation of your healing can come about by seeking His ways.

Dr. Cherry's Study Guides, Volume 2 (bound volume)

Receive thirty valuable resource study guides about topics Dr. Cherry has covered on the Trinity Broadcasting Network (TBN) program *The Doctor and the Word*.

Basic Nutrient Support

Dr. Cherry has developed a daily nutrient supplement that is the simplest to take and yet the most complete supplement available today. Protect your body daily with over sixty natural substances that fight cancer, heart disease, and many other problems. Call Natural Alternatives at (800) 339–5952 to place your order. Please mention service code "BN30" when ordering. (Or order through the company's Web site: *www.Abundant Nutrition.com.*)

Bone Support

Bone Support is a supplement that provides a broad spectrum of all the essential nutrients to guard against bone loss and enhance bone density. It supplies essential calcium along with vitamin D for proper calcium absorption and a full spectrum of nutrients, such as magnesium, trace minerals, isoflavones, and vitamin K to support the protein and connective tissue components of bone as well. Bone Support also contains a unique herbal extract called Osteogene that inhibits the breakdown of bone. Bone Support provides all the nutrients you need to build and maintain strong bones so that you can live the active lifestyle God intends for you.

Call Natural Alternatives at (800) 339-5952 to place your order. Please mention service code "BN30" when ordering.

Reginald B. Cherry Ministries, Inc.
P.O. Box 27711
Houston, TX 77227-7711
1-888-DRCHERRY

BECOME A PATHWAY TO HEALING PARTNER

We invite you to become a "pathway partner." We ask you to stand with us in prayer and financial support as we provide new programs, resources, books, pocket books, and a one-of-a-kind monthly newsletter.

Our monthly Pathway to Healing Partner newsletter sorts through the confusion about health and healing. In it, Dr. Cherry shares sensible steps, both biblical and medical, that you can take to get well. Every issue points you to your pathway to healing.

Writing from a Christian physician's Bible-based point of view, Dr. Cherry talks about nutrition and health and how to pray about specific diseases. The newsletter also includes updates on the latest medical research, Linda's own recipes for healthy eating, and questions and answers concerning issues you need to know about.

In addition, we'll provide you with Dr. Cherry and Linda's ministry calendar, broadcast schedule, resources for better living, and special monthly offers.

This newsletter is available to you as you partner with the Cherrys through prayer and monthly financial support to help expand this God-given ministry. Call or write to the following address to find out how you can receive this valuable information.

Become a pathway partner today by writing:

Reginald B. Cherry Ministries, Inc.
P.O. Box 27711
Houston, TX 77227-7711
Visit our Web site:
www.drcherry.org
1-888-DRCHERRY